Blood, Water, and Stone

Poems by
Richard Stimac

Artwork by
Ladan Bahmani
Brian Patrick Franklin

Spartan
Press

Spartan Press
Kansas City, Missouri
spartanpress.com

Copyright © Richard Stimac, 2026
First Edition: 1 3 5 7 9 10 8 6 4 2
ISBN: 979-8-89975-030-4
LCCN: 2026932650

Author photo: Anna Blomstrom
Cover image and interior art: Ladan Bahmani and Brian Franklin

"My response to *Blood, Water, and Stone* in one word: pleasure. A deep warmth that emanates from my core and lingers. With his second collection, Richard Stimac offers an intimate, generous look at what it means to be human. Personal and Midwest histories mingle with Catholic teachings and iconography, Greek mythology, the different ways water shapes the land and itself. These poems ask questions I've never thought of, yet now feel compelled to answer. I join the quest: "Who hasn't stood at the mouth of a cave, and paused?" "If even the earth cannot be trusted, how much less we?" "What then, when a river dies?" I admire Richard's craft, his invitation to love words and to love what those words convey—the self in relation to geography, history, ritual, family. Whether describing his grandmother's soup, sinkholes in the Ozarks, or a murmuration of birds, Richard's language displays an attentiveness I'm still learning. While reading this collection, I kept thinking of elegance, in the sense of a mathematical proof, and simmer, like tango. I believe these poems. I'm going where they go."

-Lynne Jensen Lampe, author of *Talk Smack to a Hurricane* (Ice Floe Press, 2022)

"*Blood, Water, and Stone* by Richard Stimac invites the reader into a total immersion in harmonious connection, where meaning gathers through history, memory, and meditation. Accompanied by the imaginative artwork of Ladan Bahmani and Brian Patrick Franklin, thecollection traces the ripples that rise from relationships between blood, water, and stone."

-Jeff Streeby, Associate Editor, *OPEN: Journal of Arts Letters*

"I've been thinking lately of poetry as the world's oldest recording device. And in this context, Richard Stimac's astonishing new collection *Blood, Water and Stone* shines forth brilliantly. You might call this book the Myth of the Midwest, for any mention of Cairo has to include our Cairo. And being St Louisans, we have little tolerance for BS—and Stimac doesn't give us any. At the outset, we're warned of the instability of river country. And a little later we hear, "I don't live in a world of metaphors." This is coming from the heart. Working through the damage that men have done, we arrive at the loving tribute of "Eucharist" and the inordinate quotidian of "Limbo." We might go all the way back to Olympia but the condition is the same: war and loss. Stimac is not quick to give easy answers, but in a poem like "Whiskey River" we can take comfort in the strength of memory. These are poems that bend toward the religious, written by someone who won't budge from his vision."

-Matthew Freeman, author of Dopamine and the Devil (Coffeetown Press 2025)

"Richard Stimac unabashedly confronts the hardest aspects of life in reverential, meticulous ways. The respect he artfully accords such a wide range of topics not only presents possible 'answers' as we try to weather this world but bestows on us hope because of the seriousness of his explorations."

-Gabe Shapiro, Retired professor of English & Journalism, Editor/Publisher of supplementstlouis.com

Acknowledgments:

Blood:

"Recipe" *Book of Matches, SHINE* (reprint); "Pastoral" *Schuykill Valley Journal;* "Ambrosia" *BeatLife;* "Bearing It" *Gargoyle, Statement* (reprint); "Memory of America" *GAS*; "My Father's Work" *Neologism, Highland Park Poetry* (reprint); "Numismatics" *NOVUS;* "Gardening" *Seventh Quarry;* "Waynesville" *Museum of Americana;* "Troubled Dreams" *LETTERS*; "Kandinsky" *Thimble;* "Jefferson Barracks" *Voices;* "Rummage" *Nova, Statement* (reprint); "Handmade" *Neolo-gism;* "Hand-me-down" *Spillwords;* "Preserves" *Sierra Neveda Review;* "Split, Croatia" *Sea to Sky;* "Late October, 1968" *Northern Eclecta, All My Poems* (reprint); "Blood Offering" *Wayne Literary Review;* "Patterns" *Steel Jackdaw;* "Plastic Fruit" *NOVUS;* "Worry Beads" *BarBar;* "Highland" *Voices, Ulu* (reprint); "Cosmetics" *Chiron;* "Currency" *Spirit Lake, All My Poems* (reprint), *The Coil* (reprint); "Eucharist" *Chiron, Writer's Digest* (reprint); "Limbo" *BarBar.*

Water:

"Down River" *Soundings East,* "Six Flags" *GAS;* "Transgressions" *The Woodside Review;* "Fishing King" *Amaranth;* "Sea is the land's edge" *Synkroniciti;* "Ephemeral Streams" *Streetlight;* "Sandbars" *Mad Swirl;* "Losing Stream" *Eunoia;* "River Blossoms" *Multiplicity;* "Tides" *LatinosUSA/ Chewers;* "Moon" *Dancing 'Neath Mr. Rucci's Moon* (Spartan Press); "Understories" *Wild Roof;* "Salvage" *Multiplicity;* "Consigned" *Freshwater, Highland Park Poetry* (reprint); "Vengeance is the sea" *Kelp;* "Desire" *As It Ought to Be, Gasconade Review* (reprint); "Geometry" *Gasconade Review;* "Confluence" *Horseshoe;* "Cairo" Sea to Sky; "Desiccation" *Hare's Paw;* "Autumn Notes" *Washington Square, Fresh Words* (reprint); "Alluvia" *The Closed Eye Open, Gasconade Review* (reprint); "Waterfalls" *Multiplicity;* "Limestone" *A Drop of the Pure* (OAC Press); "Still Water" *Eunoia;* "Whiskey River" *Rye Whiskey;* "White Washing" *SHINE.*

Stone:

"Retaining Walls" *Statement;* "Malls" *MasticadoresUSA;* "Diners" *MO Humanities magazine;* "Names" *JuxtaProse;* "Rhizomes" *Cathexis;* "Silence" *Mound City;* "Attis" *T.S. Eliot Tribute* (Moonstone); "Charnel" *Northern Eclecta;* "Mound City" *MasticadoresUSA;* "Sleeping Volcanos" *A Drop of the Pure* (OAC Press); "Flyover Dharma" *Pensive;* "Territoriality" *Borderless;* "Great American Desert" *Headlight;* "Leadbelt" *Ink, Sweat, and Tears;* "Flare" *Eunoia;* "Descansos" *SHINE* (USA), *Superlative* (UK, reprint); "Wrecking" *Verse-Virtual;* "Thomasson" *Orenaug Mountain Publishing;* "Tornado Alley" *A Drop of the Pure* (OAC Press); "Continental Drift" *Ar-lington Literary Journal;* "Counting Coup" *MasticadoresUSA;* "Field Work" *Americana* (O:JA&L); "Milkweed" *North of Oxford;* "Murmuration" *Mound City;* "Touch" *Proud to Be* (GreenTower Press); "Componere" *Line of Advance;* "Wild Violets" *Plainsongs.*

•"The Memory of America" 2024 Deane Wagner Poetry Contest Winner, St. Louis Writer's Guild

•"Names" First Prize *JuxtaProse* 2024 Poetry Prize

•"Eucharist" 19th Place 19th Annual *Writer's Digest* Poetry Awards

•"Split, Croatia" Finalist *Midway Journal* 2025 Action/ Words Poetry Contest

•"Currency" Finalist 2025 Luminaire Poetry Award (*The Coil*)

Table of Contents:

Blood

Water

Regarding the poetry and artwork:

If we accept the river as a metaphor for life, then we must acknowledge that life is unstable. We may point to a map and say, "There is the river." However, if we stand on the bank of that same river, we plant ourselves on land that will vanish when the river rises, expand when the river falls, or even dissolve as the river changes its course, something the river seldom does in a lifetime, or, at least, in a noticeable way. Over centuries or millennia, the river moves. In the past, myths conveyed these transformations. Today, with images mistaken for a fixed world, we mark time, like a mother does when she holds a family photo album on her lap and forlornly traces the growth of her children's lives and the slow decline of her own, not even the Army Corps of Engineers with its mechanical dredges and five-year plans can forestall. We have no individual lives. We are shared facts, like water, a quantity fixed from its first forming eons ago. Our lives seem bounded, but each is fed by others' tributaries, increased with floods, decreased with drought, dammed and locked, controlled by government decree for the benefit of all. None of us exist as individuals, but as collective fictions. Even our bodies will one day dissolve into their own waters, which in turn feed into another.

When my first book of poetry, *Bricolage* (Spartan Press, 2022), came out, I wanted to include original artwork, not simple illustrations. Two things stopped me from pursuing this. After five years of writing daily, I was simply tired of the book and wanted it done. Tracking down artists to work with would have been another task. Also, I was so excited that a publisher would assume the work and risk for my first book that I wanted it in production as soon as possible. I was too vain for a vanity press.

With this second book, I felt more in control of the content and the publication schedule. When I knew that I was coming to the end of collecting poems for this book, I began reaching out to local St. Louis artists. These contacts fizzled. My past experiences as a journalist and a salesperson gave me the confidence to do the legwork. I went to the St. Louis Artists' Guild for recommendations. After talking with a staff member, I didn't find anyone in the Guild who fit. I finished my visit by touring the current exhibition.

This is when I discovered Ladan Bahmani and Brian Franklin's work, which was the main exhibit at the time. Themes of transience, memory, recollection, and loss permeate my poetry. Ladan and Brian use language to explore similar themes. Much of their work included words that slowly fade. Or do they slowly appear? I liked the overall aesthetic of their work, so I emailed them. By chance, that was the last week of the exhibit. They were in St. Louis that Friday to pack up, so we had coffee. I gave them copies of the typescript and my first book. They liked them and had ideas. And here we are. Ladan and Brian's work stands alone while augmenting my work. I'd like to think my work enhances theirs.

-RS

Artists' Statement: Ladan Bahmani and Brian Patrick Franklin

The artwork accompanying the poems in *Blood, Water, and Stone* was created in response to Richard's writings, which speak with deep sensitivity to the ties between people and place. As we read the verses in this collection, we were struck by recurring themes of belonging and memory, as well as how knowledge, land, and histories are carried forward, reshaped, and often lost over time. Transformation through the tension of continuity and dissolution became central to our work.

We embraced a combination of hand and digital processes, developing a visual language that allows different methods of mark-making to coexist and interact. Hand-drawn and painted gestures hold a physical trace of the body, while digital marks and layering introduce translation and distance. As these marks accumulate, dissolve, and reform, they carve out a space where precision and ambiguity, presence and absence, overlap.

Many of the forms within the work are drawn from the geographies and architecture of St. Louis, a landscape that anchors Richard's writing. We approached these shapes not as literal maps, but as shifting contours that erode and re-form, echoing how our sense of place evolves across generations as both land and family stories are continually rewritten by time.

Each artwork is paired with a specific poem, guided by the emotions and atmospheres we experience in the verses. We aim to create spaces of reflection that live alongside the words—companions that mirror the tenderness, complexity, and shifting layers of the words in his poetry. Together, the images and poems form a conversation about how place, memory, and generational storytelling intertwine.

This collection is dedicated to anyone who is made of blood, water, and stone and to those who organize, attend, and read at St. Louis, Columbia, Rolla, Belle, and other regional readings; you remind me that there are real people behind Submittable, emails, websites, eBooks, and so on.

-RS

All of us labor in webs spun long before we were born,
webs of heredity and environment, of desire
and consequence, of history and eternity.

—William Faulkner, *Requiem for a Nun*

blood
blood
blood
blood
blood

Recipe

When I knead self-rising bread bleached so bone white
it pales my hands as if I've dug in pyre ash for relics of
     a saint,
I remember my grandma when she smoothed a bed
     sheet
atop the kitchen table then sprinkled flour across the
     threads
to keep the dough from sticking as she rolled it sheer
     as parchment
beneath the weight of the tapered pin my grandpa
     hand-lathed for her.
I stood beside her. She would pause, smile, place her
     hands on my face.

The dough smoothed from edge to edge, she cut it into
     wide strips
that looked like scrolls, then rolled them in upon
     themselves.
She held the kitchen knife with the handle smoothed
     and shined
with years of sweat and slid the blade through the folds.
With each slice, thin ribbons, long as tendons tanned
     as sutures
to bind a sheaf of folio, or a condemned man's wrists,
fell across her fingers, dusted as they were with her
     work.

Her winter pride was a watery broth glazed with
     chicken grease,
a few slivers of carrot so overcooked they dissolved
     in the spoon,
and the noodles, slight in texture, no body to test
     against the tooth,
along with black pepper shaken through the plastic
     grate of a handheld tin.
She set a cup of soup before me when I sat at her
     kitchen table,
and said, "Take this and eat. It's all I have to give.
     I'll be dead soon."
She slurped when she ate and wiped her mouth on
     her housecoat sleeve.

Only years later, when I had learned to read and write
     and speak well,
did I understand that memory lives in the mouth, as
     taste, not words.
Histories were written on those sheaves of dough,
     genealogies, traditions,
yarns spun from the American Midwest, down the
     Mississippi,
to New Orleans, to Trieste, the bottomland of the
     Danube, then where?
East? South? To the wheat fields between the Tigris
     and Euphrates?
The Horn of Africa? Each mouthful gave me a savor
     of the past.

Pastoral

Along the torn-up rail line rights-of-way,
or state highways numbered on shield signs,
you'll find small towns, most inhabited,
some not, with fallen-down filling stations,
poolhall cafes, discount small-box stores,
canted steeples, and bank clocks out of time.

Surrounded by harlequin-patches of crops,
round hay bales patterned like stone circles,
and woven fences crowned with barbed strands,
these towns persist, as much in memory as fact,
like the shadow self of the national ego,
what we desire to be yet hope we never are.

With Biblical names, like Goshen, or Bethel,
or lost tribes, Cahokia, Wabash, Illiniwek,
these towns act as living burial mounds
for our mythologies of prelapsarian ease
when men could sweat for their daily bread
and women brought forth children without care.

We all know this is how it never was.
If we dig deep enough into the ground
of any myth, we unearth dried bodies,
buried by a culture distant from us,
measured in miles, language, or time.
We long to distance ourselves

from these small towns, these ghost tracks,
the missing who never gave their names
to census takers or government agents,
the others who play the butt of jokes,
or the trope for earnest liberal empathy,
or genocide, displacement, addiction, arrest.

When any of us trace our blood into the past,
we all come from some abandoned small town
framed with straw, wattle and daub, or brick,
built along riverbanks or desert springs,
before maps fixed locations in our minds,
and the way home was only through memory.

Ambrosia

Olympic gods ate ambrosia. So, then,
marshmallow, Jello, Cool Whip, fruit cocktail?
Fried chicken, mostaccioli, corn, green beans?
On Olympus, did it never go stale?
Each year, did Hera comment on her weight
while Zeus ate his third serving of roast beef?
Demeter offer to fix you a plate?
Off-brand soft drinks? Highballs? Stag beer? Sheet-pan
cake? Either way, the chthonic gods made
the food. The distant aunts you never met
except at weddings or funerals. Not for gold,
not for fame, they fed both body and soul,
but, unlike gods, never ledgered debt.
They will live til memories of them fade.

Bearing It

You know her, one of the women, who shuffle
among the corporate desks, or down the hotel halls,
when others are at supper or a bar or asleep.

She carries for the term of her shift
the bucket and mop and toilet brush
and knowledge of those things in life

the rest of humanity prefers not to think.
She laughs with her friends at breaktime.
She smiles at the boss, wishes him the best,

and wonders where all of it goes, the dreams
of her girlhood, the desires of her soul,
the life all the fairytales promised was hers

for the having. She will not complain, but sigh,
in a way only those who have sighed with her
hear as the blues, a union of misery and of joy.

She is no Madonna. Her children are never born
Messiahs. At death, there is no resurrection
for her. She bears it and gives life to whom she can.

Memory of America

My father's body is the memory of America:
thin limbs; swollen belly; weak and resigned,
stored in an institution away from public sight.

My father's body is unexploded munitions
buried in a farmer's field. One day, a plow,
a tire, a foot will find it. We will not hear of that.

My father's body is an artifact
only academics and clinicians probe
for secrets. They will publish their findings.

My father's body is a documentary,
in many parts, shown consecutively.
Critics and viewers alike praise it.

My father's body is a family photo album.
There he is, shirtless, in a bunker near Saigon.
Here my mother, with me, in Illinois.

My father's body is a relic I contemplate.
He feels himself barely more than an object.
My father's body is the memory of America.

My Father's Work

My father returned from Vietnam
unrepentant for time he'd served

in the gangrenous canopy. He changed
out his uniform for civies in Hawaii,

by order; peace protesters assaulted soldiers.
His safety was no longer assured.

His father did his time in the same Pacific,
a field of blue with islands as stars.

The red and white of bloodied bandages
coordinated latitudes and longitudes

and his father marched for Franz Joseph
along the treeless crags of Dalmatia.

Like loaves of stone, he carried bitterness
to America, a dream to feed his children.

Fathers leave unfinished duty for sons.
Why ask of me? I took up my father's work.

Numismatics

I collected my parents' dreams
as if they were coins
scattered, absentmindedly,
across the floor.

On my knees, a supplicant,
I peered beneath their bed,
opened the Holy of Holies
of their bedroom drawers,
turned the corners of carpets
like vellum of ancient prayer books.

What I found were simple dreams:
a paid mortgage; the occasional new car;
modest vacations; bodies that did not break;
children who tried to understand,
all paid with a currency
of prayer, nostalgia, and hope.

Honestly, they were never worth much,
but I keep them in a cardboard box,
high on a shelf in the basement,
beside the furnace and sump.
I do not take them down.
No doubt, they are dull with age,
though their contours are rough,
unworn by touch.
They are not my dreams,
but I count them as my own.

Gardening

My father kept a garden,
like some men keep a mistress.
The sweat of his brow burnt his eyes
and chapped his mustached lip.
Still, he labored. As blessed as cursed,
he forced the earth to render
what it would withhold. He took
me to beds of hand-turned clay,
raised like altars above the crabgrass.
I was no helpmate. He held open
his hand and I, by instinct,
placed whatever tool he desired
in that upturned, calloused palm.
He kept for himself the why of his garden,
the drive to worry through hail,
watch leaves wilt in unseasonal heat,
toss away fruit half-eaten by squirrels.
Even in a matrix of furrows,
nature had its way with him.
As I grew older, and he grew old,
I wondered who this man was.
For all the springs, summers, falls
we bent side by side in that garden,
we spoke a handful of words,
too few to scatter in hope some grain of love
would sprout. That was not our harvest.

Waynesville

During the war, my parents owned a diner
in downtown Waynesville, not far from our trailer.
I remember little, myself being three:
two Sams, one the cook, the other a barber;
pool, pinball, darts—more than a boy could want.
I napped in a closet. My dreams were sweet.
My mom hung a crucifix with palm fronds
above the jukebox. No one noticed it.
That's how it was then, because of the war.
But there was one thing. It was '69,
'70. The diner was the bus stop
from base. They were all draftees, by that time.
In high school, they'd watched on TV the Tet
Offensive my dad fought two years before.
A bus arrived. They disembarked, a cluster
of olive drab fatigues, mesh jungle boots.
Oddly, or not, I remember no faces,
just the waist down, like a photograph cut
in half, as if amputated legs walked
of their own will, torsos, arms, and heads gone.
There was one soldier, a knife on his belt,
he knelt down, and spoke to me. I liked him.
My mother rushed from behind the register
and whisked me through the glass doors to the counter
and sat me straight on one of the round stools:
"Stay away from them," she said. "They're not good."
I understood she meant, "Not like your father,"
who dropped out of school, married, then enlisted,
all before the nation called the war bad.

Troubled Dreams

We know Joseph so little from the Bible:
his reluctance to wed; his craftsmanship
(men are their work); his devotion to God.

Were there fretful nights with a fevered son?
With silver scarce, did he forgo his bread
and watch, with joy, his daughter have her fill?

When sitting in temple, hearing Isaiah,
Ezekiel, Daniel, did Joseph fear
the end was near? How would he protect them?

Was Joseph toothless, senile, beyond wits,
when tumults in the streets disturbed his sleep,
as Romans drug criminals to their crosses?

What father hasn't had a troubled dream
of seas that rise, endlessly, and drown all,
of wars, and rapes, and body-scattered lands,

of skies that rain fire that scalds the bare skin?
Such things are not scripture. This is the news.
Not prophesy, but well-cited reports.

I remember my daughter learned of death
the day when her Syrian hamster died.
Head bowed, she held it in her upturned palms,

as I learned to take the body of Christ.
She asked, did she kill it, pet it too hard?
What did I say? What could I say to her?

We buried it shrouded in a white cloth
beneath the just-budding magnolia tree.
A late frost would burn the buds off that year.

Whatever I said to her, it was meaningless.
Performance is what makes ritual true.
I did as I had to. I was a father.

Kandinsky

My mother was an artist, of sorts, conjuring meals,
mortgage payments, Halloween costumes, Christmas

gifts from the offerings of a Catholic school salary
and odd cash from cleaning laundromats and doctors'

offices. In college, she wrote a paper on Kandinsky.
I found it, by chance, hidden among my keepsakes:

report cards; a third-grade science report; yearly
school photos. I read it. I did not understand,

at the time, how my mom's face twisted into
a portrait of ruefulness and disappointment.

As if our house were a void in her soul, she filled
it with pin-and-thread, burlap and yarn, an elongated

statue of a mother and her child. She took pride
in her work. What did I know of the bitterness

of hands that cannot make their art? I don't
have the poetry to answer. Maybe these abstract

shapes, these lines, these curves, I trace on a page
can, with imagination, represent her loss, and her gain.

Jefferson Barracks

A national cemetery rests
on bluffs above the river.
Once the largest base in the nation,
now a country park, guard depot,
and hospital. A wrought-iron
gate opens to soft curving roads.

I always thought, when driving
through, the cross-hatched rows
of the bone-white marble markers
as Hydra's teeth, hand sown
like seed spilt upon the ground
to raise a grand army of the dead.

My mother is buried there.
She will not rise, not like that,
in the least. I don't visit often,
as much as a mourning son should.
We don't miss the ones we love,
but suffer with enduring memory.

I've only been twice, in seventeen years,
once with my dad, her husband; once,
alone. He fell to his knees and sobbed.
I watched. The second time, just me,
in place of words, I threaded tears
like profane resin rosary beads

cast for the Queen of Heaven.
A doe and two fawn lazily grazed
among the stones, walking metaphors.
My God, I miss her, my mother.
She was never happy, never fully
happy. I think, at times, short-lived:

the birth of a son; her marriage;
on her deathbed, when her father,
in a vision, asked forgiveness
for the hate he bestowed on her.
Now she is dead. As we all will be.
I don't know what to make of it,

all this life, this pain, these tears,
love, loss, laughter, the heaviness
that comes with bone and skin and flesh.
May she have peace, there, among the military
dead, as if peace were a thing. I don't
live in a world of metaphors. I leave
the dead to their own eternal fate.

Rummage

Parish ladies set up their booths each fall
in the church basement, with both new and old
for trade: outdated children's clothes; or gold
glittered pinecones; an ornamental ball
of hardened popcorn; a hand-knit yarn shawl
with Mary's face; a fruitcake in the mold
of crucified Christ; if they were still sold,
indulgences, too. No suburban mall
stores such goods. But everything's not for sale,
is it? I'd like to think it's not, but know
someone, somewhere, is trying to sell love,
delivered, by air, from heaven above.
With the world's gaud, we all try to avail
ourselves of value before the first snow.

Handmade

My grandfather gave himself to his work
in wooden patterns at Commonwealth Steel.

He built his house. He gave to church. He saved.
He served in wars. He drank his beer alone.

He kept his carpenter tools in a shed
along the chain-link fence of the alleyway.

It wasn't things he built there, but himself:
end tables; kitchen stools; a rolling pin.

The practical things of life. I still have
a bookcase, the varnish worn, splintered legs,

no nails, pure joinery, where parts just fit.
Who knows the fruit of the labor of men?

Hand-me-down

I hang my memories on the brittle branches
of a Christmas tree. I never tire of the yearly ritual
exhuming the cardboard box from the basement.
I brush the collected dust with solemnity and unfold
crisscrossed flaps to expose the remains of the past:
an elf of multi-colored yarn scissored,
bound into arms and legs and head;
oven-baked clay in the shape of a stubby snowman
with hand-drawn eyes, nose, mouth;
a silver-glittered pinecone with each scale
like the petals of a nebula saturated with stars;
a nativity-themed Hallmark card hole-punched
for thread strung through; garlands of tinsel
snake around the trunk like a serpent
sneaking through a walled garden;
a string of colored lights, the old kind,
where you had to test each to find the broken circuit.
There is a pattern to follow, a sequence,
what is first, what is last, what is done in between.
But nothing is written. There is no missal of liturgy
with prescribed prayer and gesture.
I work by memory, of what my mother taught me,
and her mother her, the way things are
to be done. Yet, I admit, each year,
the order of things changes, though I am certain
I remember exactly what I did the year before. I trust
    myself that what I think
is my past, my memory, my life, is my past, my
    memory, my life.

Otherwise is chaos. It's not written word,
but speech, action, example, that makes a life.
With repetition, no new year is ever new. In the end,
I wait too long, far past New Year's Day, when I reintern
these hand-me-downs and set the yellowed cardboard box
on the same basement shelf for another season,
another winter solstice, another remembering.

Preserves

Behind the veneer-skinned hollow-core door of a sheetrock room, more a basement closet than walk-in cellar, rows of Mason jars filled with tomatoes, peaches, beets, green beans, and okra grin from plywood shelves like skulls stacked in the hand-carved catacombs of ancient ossuaries, objects of remembrance not of mortality but reminders that our acts persist beyond our deaths and blesséd are the ones who know the rites and rituals that preserve memories that persist through the starving seasons of our lives and feed our hunger in our times of need.

Split, Croatia

My grandpa and uncle took me to Split,
their first family heritage trip abroad.
After the coast, we went inland, to Brod-
na-Kupi, ate lamb roasted on a spit,
dipped pogacha in rendered fat. We'd sit,
sip slivovitz, til both old men would nod
to sleep. At that age, I didn't know how odd
those two together were. The casting pit
of the foundry cleaved them. My grandpa stayed
union. His brother took a foreman's role.
For years, they never spoke, at the KC,
sat at opposing ends of the bar, and paid
their bitter debt, failed to reckon the toll.
Now, old, sick, they let their resentment be.

Late October, 1968

I was born on a farm in Illinois,
at 6 am. It was 41 degrees
in late October, 1968.

The doctor counted it out for my mom.
Ten fingers. Ten toes. Plus one. It's a boy
in late October, 1968.

The kitchen radio announced corn
dropped to barely a dollar a bushel
in late October, 1968.

The Vietnam monthly death toll approached
a total nearing five hundred, so far,
in late October, 1968.

My dad made his berth in a Quonset hut
thirteen kilometers from Tan Son Nhut
in late October, 1968.

Two black men, Smith and Carlos, lost their medals
with five fingers, not one, raised in the air
in late October, 1968.

NASA sent three more astronauts to space
on Apollo 7, live on TV,
in late October, 1968.

Nixon beat Humphrey by under one point,
but led in the polls by well over five
in late October, 1968.

Poverty levels of thirteen percent,
one in eight persons, began to decline
in late October, 1968.

The total Vietnamese dead was
tough to measure, by all official means,
in late October, 1968.

I didn't know how many numbers there were
in the world, or how little I could count on,
in late October, 1968.

Blood Offering

When it comes to women's blood, there is no cult
of mothers slit from perineum to manubrium.
Their afterbirth is enough to spare their lives.

Nor, in lore, do we find impaled grandmothers,
their bodies returned to pre-pubescent proscription,
age its own salvation from the touch of a man.

Instead, we find the blood of virgins, led, in hand,
by father, brother, uncle, or priest, along a staircase
either to a sundrenched altar atop a pyramid,

or along torchlit cavern walls. What did she think
as a man she trusted with her life ordered what to wear,
where to stand, or sit, or kneel, or look away?

In Rome, when the last brick was mortared in place,
did the sweaty mason set his ear against the wall
to hear the faint moans of the un-virgined Vestal

as she plowed her fleshless fingertips across the
     courses?
Did the stains of blood resemble the streaked mascara
of a debutante jolted by her homecoming beau?

In Cahokia, beside the hierophant's platform, a mound
risen above the ox-bow lake and ranks of corn, bodies
of girls raised a cairn, one atop the other, strangled,

or bludgeoned, to accompany a great man beyond death,
or ensure a rich harvest or well-balanced trade or peace
along the Father of Waters. The city collapsed in decades.

How do we take Gianna Molla, who laid herself
like an atoning lamb across the starched white sheets
of a hospital bed, to deliver herself as an oblation?

Did her pain, and her prayer, unstain her body,
reseal her labia from the lustful gaze of men?
Like Jesus, was she her own sin offering?

The history of civilization is the history of men,
at money and at war, at power and at violence,
all to hide that primal fear of a woman's body.

Patterns

So many women make lives reproducing
patterns, weaving weft and warp of life
into images new yet somehow known.

In Sais, Lower Egypt's western delta,
Nit rewove the world each night, a world birthed
from her heart, alone, virgin as she was.

On Andes eastern slopes, Mama Ocllo
taught Inca to spin thread, to weave a cloth
to cover the body from mountain frost.

On her western island, Penelope
undid her daily work, unstitched the thread
the merciless Moirai measured each soul.

The Valkyrie used human heads as loom weights;
entrails as thread; swords, shuttles; arrows, reels.
These women bore death to the men they'd bed.

We are all fashioned by filaments woven
with and within the bodies of our mothers,
until the thread is ripped out, the cord rent.

My mother? My mother only made clothes.
She pinned gray pattern tissue to work cloth,
then traced the template lines with pinking shears.

In my unraveled manhood, I reproduce
stitched, uneven lines of images, darning
my own feminine patterns. We all do.

Plastic Fruit

My grandma kept plastic fruit in a Pyrex bowl
on her linoleum kitchen table with rusted metal legs.

On one wall, above the fridge, a crucifix and brown
    fronds;
opposite, graven image to graven image, a Kit-Kat
    Clock.

His head cocked to the side, Jesus' eyes were forever
    cast downward;
the Kat's eyes darted back and forth in constant
    scrutiny.

The rueful eternal turned away from the vigilant
    temporal.
In summers, Grandma would pour us sugary milk
    coffee

and break hardened Christmas cookies onto gold-
    lined platters.
We dipped the cookies into the coffee, then we ate
    and drank.

One day, I remember, the windows open, white crepe
    curtains
fluttered in the breeze, reaching, then falling, over
    and over.

She went to nap. Like a high priest before the tabernacle,
I set the plastic fruit on the cold oven racks. They did
    not melt.

Still, when she rose, I hid in the ash-grey gravel alley.
She called me. I did not answer. She called a second time.

Again, I was silent. She called a third time. Like a ram's
    horn,
the low moan of a passing freight shook both heaven
    and earth.

I returned after dusk. She sat at her linoleum table with
    its plastic fruit,
a rosary in one hand, a forgiveness I could never earn
    in the other.

Worry Beads

I remember her devotion, her murmur
of prayer, her beatitude, her smile,

as if in the act of praying, she saw
the magnificent glory of heaven

as her taut fingers worried her rosary.
This was her afternoon obligation.

She would heat a pan of her thin soup
and set out a bowl for each of us.

Beads of grease drifted like clouds
across the surface, in its own way,

an infinite sky, an un-bordered world.
As she ate, she hummed, just as she did

when I was a small child, in her arms,
a thread of nonsense syllables

pregnant with more meaning than all
the sacred texts of all the beatified saints.

What did she mean? I string these words
into lines, a vain attempt to answer mystery.

Highland

No longer a young man,
I go east from the Gateway Arch,
that monstrous portal to the West,
a monument to destruction and glory,
empire and enslavement, to all the good

and bad my country offers. To me,
the prairie has a sacredness,
the unadorned vistas of the sky
remind me of gods: Zeus,
Azman, even Yahweh, on high.

I've come to visit my father,
in a nursing home, in Highland,
with its shuttered church
organ company, microbrewery
on the square, coffee shops, and more,

where my earthly father
has come to slowly die, dissolve,
like morning mist. Each time I visit,
less and less of him is there,
in Highland, Illinois.

I wonder at him, that he even lived.
I know his haunts: the alleys
behind the mill; the linoleum halls
of a now-demolished grade school;
a photo of him, shirtless, in Vietnam.

And now this. His teeth fall out.
He wants me to sue the home.
He tells me the same war stories.
I smile. He's not happy, but
content, which may be the same.

We don't hug goodbye. Haven't
in decades ever touched. He turns up
the TV with reruns of Bonanza.
I watch Highland fade in my mirrors.
I want to cry, to feel the loss.
Rain begins. Heaven cries for me.

Cosmetics

She sat in front of her vanity and put on her face,
piece by piece. Foundation. Primer. Concealer.
Like a priest, she placed herself before the mirror
and performed this daily ritual of transubstantiation.
With cosmetics, she solidified her sanity
and cemented her place and kept the cosmos in order.

As a boy, transfixed, I sat beside her
and watched my mother become a woman
I did not recognize. Often, she wore only
a bra and underwear. Her nipples pressed
through the lace. Her pubic hair pushed
beyond the cloth. Her body was not mine.

She did as much to placate my father
who liked his woman to be a woman.
"There's a hole in my heart," he claimed,
"only my wife can fill." He felt less
a man when she let herself go. "Just be
the woman I need," he prayed. She answered.

Now, for me, as a man, what mask do I wear?
For sexual play, there must be another.
A missing second voice is a soliloquy.
Monologue requires an audience. A lacking
defines my soul, an emptiness I fill with words
that disappear, as my mother did behind her face.

Currency

Buried in the back of the family safe,
itself cornered in the side hallway closet
behind my mom's dresses and old board games,
boxes of worthless gold coins gathered dust.
They weren't completely worthless, but worth less,
far, far less, than what my dad paid for them.
He was a sucker for TV coin shows
with their proof grades, mint states, and troy ounce
    weights,
words with density that lent gravitas
to buy-now deals and prices guaranteed
to rise like stock markets, or one's net worth.
My dad didn't buy coins so much as a dream
he could best the guy next door, or a friend.
We're all elitist in some common way.
For me, the oddest thing about the coins
was that they were sold in a plastic case,
like incorrupt saints you find under glass
in quaint frescoed chapels stumbled upon
when lost in the twisted streets of a borgo,
or princesses asleep beneath cut crystal,
their bodies unstroked by the hands of men.
In all three cases—woman, coin, and saint—
human touch devalues the human-made.
A fetish must be worshipped from afar;
to be divine, a god must stay transcendent.
My dad now lays in a mechanized bed,
his arms and legs skeletal, shaking hands,
distended stomach below heaving ribs,

bewildered eyes, mumbled speech that runs back
against itself, in circles, without end,
a flattened pillow haloing his head.
He is my transi; I, his supplicant.
But there is not, at the foot of his pallet,
a candle, angel of grief, or mite box
for me to drop two bits of copper coin,
light a wick, whisper formulary prayer,
cross myself, then return to days of work.
Soon, soon, me and my brother will unrack
our mother's clothes, sweep the dust, one last time,
then sell those gold coins alloyed with the dreams
they were meant to buy, but only on loan.
We will sell them, to a dealer in specie,
divide the gain, and think of them no more.

Eucharist

If the countertops were an altar's *mensa,*
the kitchen sink, an empty *sepulchrum,*
hung cabinets, hallowed tabernacle,
then my grandma was the blessèd celebrant.
On metal folding tables in the basement,
she set out offerings of ham, roast beef,
sausage, fried chicken, lamb kabobs, and sides
of three-bean salad, coleslaw, ambrosia.
"Do this in remembrance of me," she meant
when she said, "This time next year, I'll be dead."
We would laugh. She would, too. And then we ate.
That went on for years, until she did die.
Now, when I make a plate at some potluck,
I pause. Remembrance is its own thanksgiving.

Limbo

It was never official doctrine of the Church,
this place of little pagan babies, an eternal womb,
without positive punishment for unearned sin.

Some punishments are what you do not receive.
As children, my parents adopted their own lost infants.
What did they know, how they would be unredeemed,

their own limbo, that liminal space that edges Hell,
the time between a paycheck and a mortgage due,
the wait from a medical test to its result,

the gap midway between a government form and an
    answer?
You don't have to die without baptism to be caught
in the netherworld. That part the Church got wrong.

water
water
water
water
water

Down River

When Fred Hampton went south,
did he follow Illinois Route 3,

first past Alton, where Lincoln
begged the question of slavery,

and Lovejoy lay in an unmarked grave,
past the rotted stockade of Lewis and Clark,

the marker for the 1814 Hartford Massacre,
past East St. Louis and its riotous blues,

the broken ankh of the Gateway Arch,
the abandoned mounds of Cahokia,

past Kaskaskia and Fort de Chartres
where the French hugged the river

just as the Great River Road does today,
past all the past, until he stopped at Menard

with its brown limestone below the bluffs
above the thick soil of the black bottom?

He never reached deep into Little Egypt,
not to Cairo, nor the temples of Memphis

where the Cherokee crossed to the other side,
where the Ohio widens the Mississippi,

where Jim missed his turn in the dark mist of night.
Neither man made it to the Promised Land.

Six Flags

There were six flags out front of Six Flags,
one for each nation-state's claim of ownership.

Inside the gate (re-entry was free), minstrels sang
"Camptown Races." None of them danced

on the concrete false cobblestone street
along a facade of 19th-century storefronts.

To the right, a pair of lawn jockeys stood picket
before the path to the miniature Model-Ts.

The Log Flume made everyone wet
past cardboard pine trees not yet clearcut.

The Mine Train thrust deep into the earth
for gold, coal, copper, what did it matter?

On the Buccaneer, all the pirates were dark,
as if the Barbary migrated to Bermuda.

A French log stockade fired cannon
at the River Boat. A canoe of Indians

crept from a blind, then retreated.
And then Injun Joe's Cave, a tunnel

of love redone apropos Mark Twain.
That's where the boys of Mary

Magdalene assaulted the girls. It was
enough to make Injun Joe blush.

He was quite a character. In a novel way,
we read the same stories today,

but, now, we are told they are true,
which makes them harder to believe.

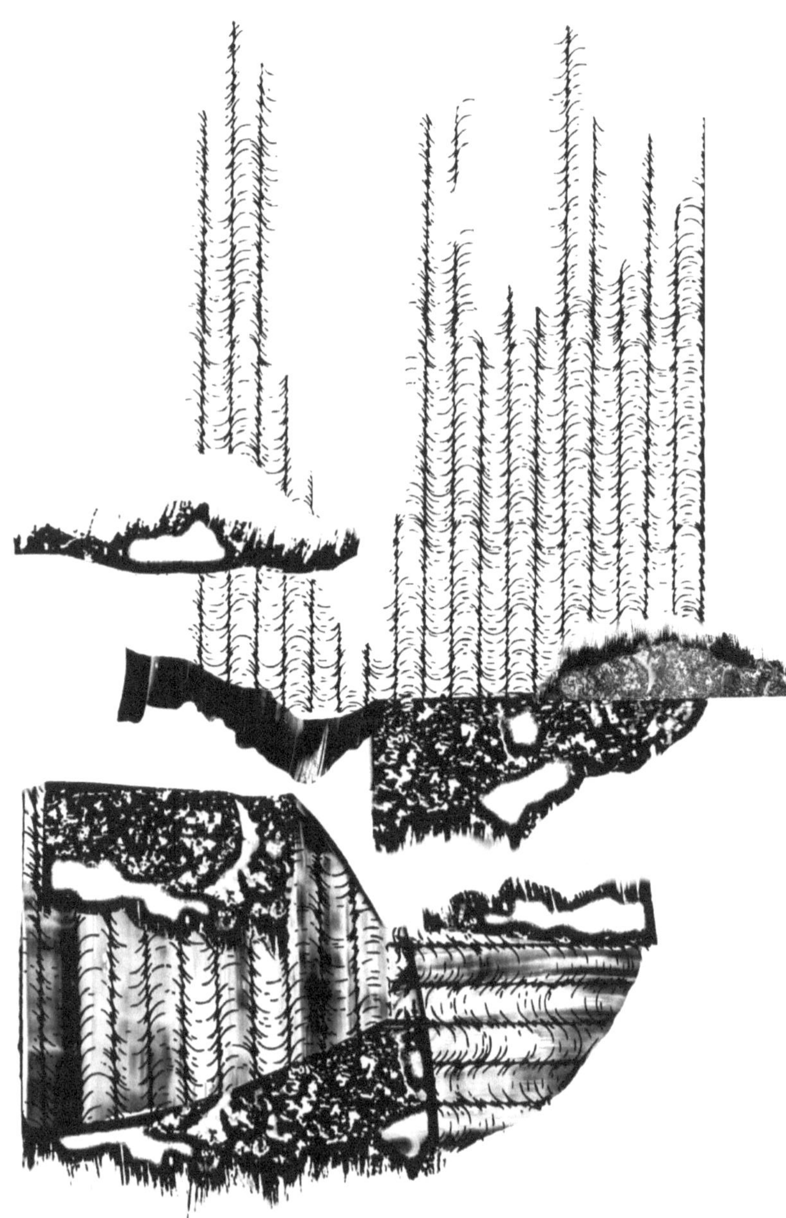

Transgressions

At one time, the sea cleaved this continent in two,
From Gulf to Arctic. The ancient Appalachians
and the adolescent Rockies embraced this marine
    transgression
as if the mountains were a mother's arms, the shallow
    salty water, her newborn.

Slowly, today, the sea reclaims delta and floodplains.
Chaos, if chaos exists, returns to the platted land.
Maps must be redrawn. Values recalculated.
Entropy is perspective, not fact.

Can the edge of land and water ever be measured?
The now between past and present?
The sea reminds us, we never know exactly where we are,
where we begin, where we end. Nothing is liminal,
if the limits are always in play.
Disorder is a new order, unwanted and inevitable.

This is how I see the body:
we have no borders; we know no restraints.
Certainty is a self-portrait, a fixed moment, a chart
we reference when we forget who and where we are.
Even our skin erodes like coast lines slough
into the eternal break of waves.
Yet we fear the dissolution of the self.

The sea will rise. We know that.
We will die. We will be forgotten.
But like river silt, or inundated coasts,
parts of us continue. Someone may point
to a map, history book, family album, and say,
here he is, submerged now. Or,
there she once lived, before the flood. Or,
a great structure built by human hands once stood
where now the tidal force teases,
where mudflats bloom and wilt twice a day.

I should have solace, in knowing, I am a forever thing.
But the soft surf, rhythmic, gentle, like the heartbeat
of a mother, does not comfort me. I long to stand,
    alone,
on the shore, look to the sea, ponder the infinite,
shrouded in a rainproof windbreaker.
The sea reflects the sky. The sky reflects the land.
They both reflect upon me.

Fishing King

King cast his nets in the violet hour,
early morning, when the sun refracted
indigo through the floating kish,
and the blast furnace bleeding line
flared with ghostly blues and whites.

Built to dump the coking plant's clinker,
Dead Run flowed behind the mill.
King would plant his lawn chair and rod
atop the levee. The canal once caught fire.
TV crews from worldwide took footage.

At this distance, once the yellow fog lifted,
the barges appeared like gilded shells.
Some dawns, the glint of metallic dust
across the arid abandoned fields
forced his sweaty face to smile.

Some would call his life oppressed,
and if pressed, he might agree, a touch.
But he knew, the opposite of oppression
is not freedom, but depression. To live
with desire requires restraint. That is all.

Old, sterile, a widower, and poor,
he washed his feet in the water slick
with oil and tar. In the sunrise, the city,
far to the west, seemed unreal. He ground
the carp into patties and fried them in lard.

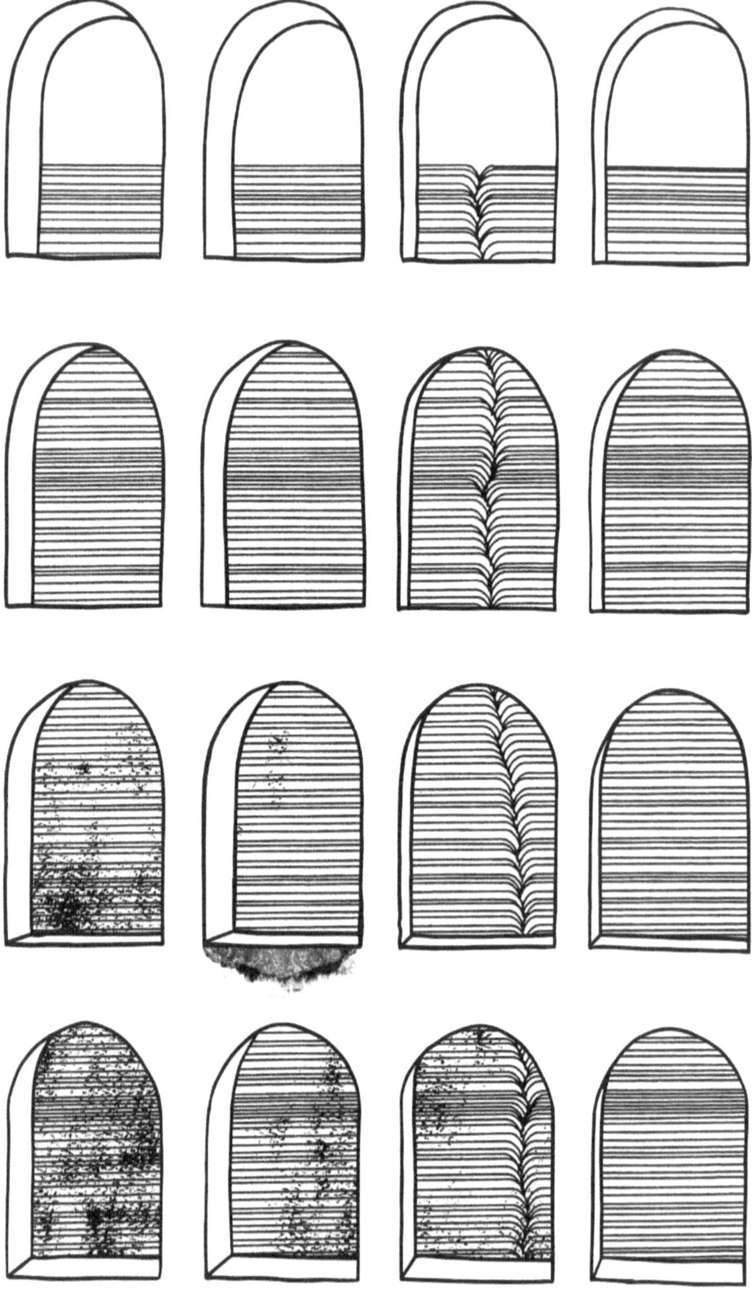

"Sea is the land's edge"

Here, in the Midwest, we are far
from the plaintive song of the sea,
so we think. Though what is the river
but the remnants of a shallow sea?
The poet tells us the river
cuts a deep valley through the soul.
Imagine that, the river, a brawny god
who swings a chisel of hewn flint
and cleaves a chasm down the breast
from headwater to the delta between our legs
where all things empty into unfathomed tides.

Those are romantic and comforting thoughts,
like a rhythmic nursery rhyme a mother sings
her frightened child, or the solace of a priest,
conflicted between compassion and creed,
as he strokes the hand of a man
dying, but unrepentant. What does one do?

I, for certain, do not know.
Very seldom, often drunk, or high, or both,
I let my imagined self float on the current,
a desire to be free from desire.
The deep, knowing waters take me
where they want me to go.
In my imagination, so I am.

But in the real, the river is filthy
with industrial waste and fertilizer
and the undecayed discards that ground
the street, the house, the frame,
all the structure of what makes life
life, as we live it. And so, too, this to the sea.

Which leaves us, where?
We are eternal and bound,
we are the earth, and the map
imposed upon it. The river
is always silent, but if you listen,
as I do, you can hear the whisper
of waves as they wear down the shore.

Ephemeral Streams

If the river is a metaphor for life and death,
for time, and loss of time,
for the rise and fall of seasons,
for disastrous floods that carry hope downstream
and leave stinking mud in its place,
what then, when a river dies?

You can see the river from atop
concrete steps with granite tread that lead
from the cobblestone along the current's edge
to the manicured grass and pruned trees of federal land
beneath the stainless-steel legs of the Arch.
The Museum of Westward Expansion is closed for
    renovation.

This river was once the artery of a continent,
carrying both mound builders and mound destroyers,
wampum from the east, slaves to the south,
Jesuits from the Great Lakes, conquistadores from the Gulf
who the Natchez chased through the delta.
Black Hawk crossed from west to east, then back.

One does not need a Hollywood-handsome Moses,
red Levite robe, arms outstretched, staff in right hand,
to enter the river now. There is a third of dry land
on either side, like plaque narrowing the flow.
The Army Corps keeps the channel nine feet.
That is all the depth the nation needs.

Forecasters predict storms over the land,
in the near future, not enough to refill the river.
History never turns back against itself.
The river, we can see, may resurrect, and flood.
The metaphor, our nation's soul, that river, I fear,
may be too low, too ephemeral, too dry to revive.

Sandbars

At the corner of the confluence, in a small state park,
after months of drought, when the river depth
    shallowed,
I stood on a sandbar, as if I were Moses, and Yahweh,
in His Heavenly Host, began to part the merging waters
between Illinois and Missouri so His enslaved children,
carrying what they possessed, and the weight of history,
could flee from bondage. God left His work unfinished.
I write my own scripture of this. No one will read my
    verse
as mythology. I know natural fact from constructed
    fiction.

But what to make of this river, shrunken in its power,
its majesty, its commerce, frontier, and mystery?
If the river is a god, then our god is moribund,
though no one can yet walk from bank to bank.
The river still divides us, as each word divides
the named and the unknowable.

At dusk I turned away from the river to the west,
and seemed to look unblinded into the sun. Its refraction
hung just above the tips of trees that in silhouette
look like fingers reaching heavenward.
What I saw was a harmless illusion.
Rangers would swing the metal gates closed soon.

I retreated in my car then down a paved county road,
to the Interstate, past the airport, to home,
where metaphors are abstractions on the page
and history confines itself to books.

Losing Streams

An empire of karst holds sway beneath the Ozarks.
Rainwater wore away limestone and dolomite.
Sunless passages meander beneath the plateau.

At times, the earth gives way and sinkholes expose
what no human eye has yet seen. Or springs
remit horded rainwater that feeds stream,

then river, then sea. But, sometimes, this blue water
longs for its darkness, or the caves yearn
for the wearing touch of water. Desire

is like this: does the void subsume the object,
or the object pervade the void? I wander
through my own dark landscape, my spirit

like water that both shapes and is shaped by its
form. In the symbolic order of the sun,
I evaporate. Soon I will be no more.

So, I, too, return to a sightless, unnamable world,
colorless, and quiet, measured in eons.
I, too, have an empire of karst in my soul.

River Blossoms

The river blooms into the Gulf.
We see satellite images of bloody petals
push their way open, like a carnation
hanging limp in the ocean-blue sky,
with all its silt of cracked quartz
and all the factory-made fertilizer.

The lower river is the stem,
the Missouri, the Ohio, rhizomes
that thrust their way into the heart
of the country. Once a salty expanse
covered the land. When this sea retreated,
it left the rivers as its remains.

It is we who have sown this seed,
turned the earth over, against itself,
until this flower of evil buds.
The pus drains into the watershed,
like gangrene. Surgeons will amputate
the continent county by county.

Listen to the slow purr of the surf
as it slowly devours the coast.
It will come, this beast, and grind
with its teeth the alluvial lands.
That flower will never fruit,
but in time it will go to seed.

Tides

The moon does not cause tides
to rise and fall. The water is still.
The earth turns inside the bulging sea.
We move but confuse our place as stable.

But what do I know of tides, born here,
a thousand river miles from the mouth?
Our waters rise and fall with seasons,
not hours. We measure days with the sun.

We were once the solid, unchanging ones,
in the heart of the country. Our rivers,
its arteries. To know the soul of the country
was to go west, but only so far. We were the end.

Now the coasts control the nation
with people who see themselves
as the measure of tides, unaware
they are as unstable as we of the plains.

It is said the coasts will fall into the sea,
go deep into the water, until they disappear.
What then of us, rent in two, like the sail
of a floundering ship caught in a tempest?

Like the arms of a mother, the mountains
will keep the tide at bay, until the shallows
of the Gulf rise, as they did once before,
and we, too, find ourselves drowned.

Moon

Who doesn't love poems about the moon?
Or verse on constellations of the stars?
Even atheists read poems on heaven.
Materialists grow tired of the earth.
Things like sick children, bills, wars lack the gravity
to turn our eyes from shadows to the sun.

I go to the park in summer and sun
myself to golden brown, and love to moon
over fantasies of peace, like the stars,
there, but hidden in the day, as if heaven
were nothing more than to lay on the earth
and let my body bear the weight of gravity.

I've read there's only consensus on gravity,
sole effect, no proof. It seems the sun
bends our space and our time more than the moon.
Size, not distance, gives power to our stars.
That's how it is with everything in heaven:
it's we who give weight to the things on earth.

If angels, in fact, did visit the earth,
they'd find in us a lack of classic gravity,
we, who think we've seen all under the sun,
and, Christ's sake, nothing new under the moon.
We measure life with pop charts, movie stars,
clothing store sales. Consumption is our heaven.

When I buy quinoa at The Gate of Heaven,
an old hippy store, once called Sacred Earth,
the store clerk, long white beard, spine bent by gravity,
always tells me, "Be grateful for the sun."
That's it. Never, "Be grateful for the moon."
He nurtures a prejudice for the stars

in me. I prefer the moon over stars.
Honestly, I favor earth over heaven,
though, in familiarity, the earth
is more like prose, the words with too much gravity.
Not poetry, where words hide from the sun,
give meaning like the shadow of the moon.

I love the moon over the stars in heaven,
earth over the gravity of the sun.

Understories

My country is the confluence of Mississippi and
    Missouri,
the river country of once submerged granite cliffs
to bottomland of black soil and understory of rot.

The river creates this land. Sediment abrades bedrock.
Floods shroud lowlands with silt.
The river is both creation and creator.

We even count time with the Big Water:
"One Mississippi. Two Mississippi."
As if our words create yearly change.

Springs from subterranean lakes birth new rivers.
Stones, cloven like the skull of a god,
give rise to springing headwaters.

That is why we worship them, with their innate
    wisdom.
In our abysmal fear of oblivion, we know
rivers submit as oblates to the holy sea.

The two great rivers flow side by side for miles
beyond the confluence. The rust-brown,
the jaundice-yellow, meld to putrid-green.

They are like lovers, determined to follow separate paths,
but drawn by laws of nature to touch, tentatively,
avoid coupling, then, lose identity in inevitable union.

Sex and death flow side by side, too. In our imagination,
we keep them separate, as if we were engineers
of the soul able to raise levees, construct dams

that limit the terrible destruction of bed and grave
immersed beneath us. We do not so much
drown as we sink, like sand, to the bottom.

In the last legs of the journey, we rest in the delta,
the open mouth of the river, as it spews
its discharge, a continent worn down by friction,

into the salty, seemingly infinite expanse of the sea.
For us, anything greater than a river is infinite.
We all come from a country of rivers.

Salvage

Captain Eades walked the murky river bottom
in a pitched whiskey barrel weighted with lead.

A thin rubber tube brought air from above.
Hand over hand, he groped his way

through the mud until his fingers hooked
a balustrade, or fetter links, or jagged edges

of a boiler's burst copper plates.
He'd clasp a chain and haul the chattel up.

Returned to the sun, he laid like a corpse
on the deck of the boat. His body ached. He labored

for breath. He grew sleepy. And still he searched
for wrecks. When a boy, his family landed

on the cobblestone wharf. The ship caught fire.
Everything they owned sank. Within years,

his father escaped upriver. The family lived
in poverty. By thirty, Eades made a fortune.

He waged war against the river all his life.
I, too, dived the wrecks, hidden in darkness.

When I was a boy, we lived on a raft
of American dreams and union paychecks.

The bargemen piled cords of torrefied bones in the tender.
Tears of condescension wept down the furnace flue.

We felt our gears slip. The current proved
too strong. The river, like all sleeping gods, devours

its young. When we sank, my father lost
his health, then his ambition. My mother's

body dissolved on laundromat floors
and doctor's waiting rooms. My brother,

too young to know, feared why
gifts were so few. I threw my goods

overboard and swam for the feral bank.
We stood wet and cold and penniless

along the landing. My father fell to bed.
My mother, to work. My brother, to his machines.

And I, to words, my salvage, the ruined hulk
hidden below the waves. I've dived deep.

Lightless, I groped water-logged photo albums,
cribs crusted in sludge, tract homes smeared

with the soot from mills, cars driven to rust,
unused food stamps, bonuses, like deferred happiness,

and bodies, like ghosts, but not, of what
might have been, deluged of dreams.

I let such images recede. No underwriter desired
to pay me specie to haul this junk to light.

Some things are best left unclaimed, sunken
in the sands of time. Let some future

treasure hunter test his worth against the current.
I turn my back on wealth. I am poor in things.

Consigned

I use my cracked coffee cup with its broken
handle, bowed wooden spoon, stained dinner plate,
those home goods most of us sell for a token
price, donate to Goodwill, or, at any rate,
apologize for when we have a guest.
I can't help but love things that arouse hate.
Nothing comforts like a threadbare armrest,
or thin-soled shoes, or holey underwear.
The end of things always leaves me depressed.
When life breaks into pieces, and despair
spills across warped laminate kitchen floor,
with pan and brush, my ritual, my prayer,
I save the past's shards and flakes. I adore
the lost. Who needs a future? Who needs more?

Vengeance is the Sea

Like a sea monster risen from the depth,
a hulking beast of trash twists against itself.
Ground infinitudes insinuate in our food,
our drink, our breath. We become what we discard.

Entropy exists in chartered corporate waters
while governments map plans for remediations.
We are at the end of history. The future is cancelled.
There is no end but the endless repetition of today.

I am haunted by a vision of the sea
that once covered all the earth.
Retreating with the waters was the Goddess
of Vengeance: Furies, Kali, Leigong.

Once cathedrals rose to Mary, minarets to Allah,
stupas to Buddha, ziggurats to Ishtar.
Today, conglomerates rebrand, like chattel,
the faculties of human thought and freedom.

There is no revelation to be had.
Vengeance has come to rest.
She is a Leviathan beached
upon a desolate strip of sand

to labor with divine birth pangs.
But the Messiah is stillborn.
Like a salty tide forever rising,
this Maria pursues bitter retribution.

I see it, in satellite photographs,
more clearly in my soul, this transgressing
sea as it slowly devours the coasts.
It is not dust but the sea to which we return.

Desire

You'd think something like a river is a fixed thing.
Maps, no matter how old, keep rivers in the same place.
Names change. Boundaries move, or dissolve.
Arrows mark migrations and invasions.
The river, given erosions and sediment, stays the course.

All adults are really children fixated with desire.
All things change, with time. This is a truism.
But some things change so slowly, so easily unnoted,
we assume them permanent and build our imagination
    around them.
To think things can be otherwise is to be a god.

That was the first sin, in the Land Between the Rivers.
The Serpent implanted an aphorism in Eve: "What if?"
Eden could be different than it was. Paradise lost with
    options.
Wisdom is knowing all that is need not be all there
    can be.
After the Fall, we could no longer accept we simply are.
    Like the river,

that once enclosed Paradise, and now slowly dies in its
    way
to the delta, I turn against myself. I am not enough.
Or so I feel. Like the river never rests in its mindless
    meander,
through my works, my days, wants and grasps, kisses,
    goodbyes,

I long to be a fixed thing, without movement, without
    will and thirst,

to be a standing body of water, a lake, a pond, a
    flippant backyard pool.
But that's not true. It's the sea I fear, the end of
    course, when all the sediment
collected over a continent dissolves into salt water.
    There the river ends.
The maps lose their contour. Far at sea, we lose our
    landmarks.
Lost, we drift, and lift our heads to the stars, secure
    in their heavens.

Geometry

We are the earth, platted and plotted, and allocated.
And the sea, the relentless, unconscious sea,
as we know, from department statistics and bureau
    reports,
these dark, wide, silent waves encroach and reclaim the
    land, reclaim us,
until all we thought solid, soaked with our sweat, buried
    with our dead,
our blood percolated to aquifers,
all that dissolves, and, behind it, allots
forests of grey trees and abandoned homes
hung on stilts, as if we could flee from the future.
We know this will happen.
This we cannot prevent.
In some ways, it should be solace,
that from the dust of the earth,
the silt of the river, we have come,
to the lightless bed of the sea, we will return.

Confluence

The state piled a cairn at the conflux.
A brass plaque reminisces
about Lewis and Clark. Unnamed:
mound builders, underground railroads,
massacres, bridges and barges,
floods, all the give and take of the river,
too facile, too predictable a metaphor.
Next to the pile of rocks are benches.
On the opposite bank, a concrete tower
grants a heaven-eye view of the currents,
one brown-gray, the other orange-yellow.
They wait to merge for miles,
like lovers, afraid to touch.

Last time I walked that trail
along the strand, the river retreated,
not from me, too insignificant,
but from itself, drought-sunk
to record lows. The sky withheld
rain for a year. Groynes of granite
stretched across dry sand.
Both should be submerged.
The land is transgressing
into a river that has lost its fight.
Not even the Corps can save it.

Cairo

When I passed Thebes, I prayed my pilgrimage
to Cairo purged my soul, and I would sink,
like dissolved sand, into the ancient river

that wore away the banks of fields of grain,
wetlands, and hamlets with homes raised on stilts
in Illinois' uneven southern tip.

But all I found were taverns with slot machines,
church-windows boarded with plywood, and charred
Victorian homes of once rich boatmen.

A week of rain led the floods to rush the walls
of earth and concrete that surrounds the town.
Walls keep out floods, not its metaphor, time.

I expected history to greet me,
guide me through times of flat-keeled riverboats
with gambles, New Orleans musicians, priests

and prostitutes. There were also two lynchings.
White and black, each. There's a photo online.
Dickens used Cairo as an ideal hell.

The past is foreign land with its own myths,
folktales, lore, scriptures to unknown gods
we imagine we can take as our own.

I did meet history, poor, rural, sad,
not colorful, like movies, where it's clean,
fun, and safe, the violence, choreographed.

At the end of the day, my soul did sink,
as if rotting driftwood ripped through its bottom,
and currents pulled it to the mud below.

Desiccation

The great rivers of the Midwest have gone dry.
Sections of grain burn beneath the August sun.
Seasonal floods refuse to follow their time.

This summer, the earth cracks like the thin, dry skin
of the old. In winter, the soil freezes to the touch,
as if the circulation has gone out of it.

The earth is in its dementia. If we make this land
our mother, how can a child witness the decline
of the womb that bore it, the breasts that gave suckle?

Our bodies are the true lands of our birth.
If from dust we came, to dust we return,
then, when all is dust, what have we become?

Alluvia

We are river dust,
undulating silt of sand, clay,
broken pieces of quartz.
Floods birth us. When the river
sloughs its lining and deposits
its burden across the American Bottom,
the river, potent mother, carries us
to term, saves us from cross-bedded
deltas, then dissolving salty seas.

Autumn Notes

When the show is over, the lights come on,
the crowds have gone their way, the band leaves notes
windfallen across the sole-worn dance floor.

I glean the seed-sized quarters, halves, and wholes,
destem their staves, and strip the leafy flags,
before I drop them in my drawstring mesh

and tote them home to core and peel and press
for cold fermented cider, brandy, mead.
I age my memories of music well.

Waterfalls

We heard but never saw
the rush of the woodland stream
over an outcrop of limestone.
The stream marked the boundary
between our land above the bluffs
and the swath for the state highway
the county maintained. Below,
farms covered the bottom.
Beyond was the river.

Heavy weekend rains flooded the road.
We couldn't drive to Sunday mass
so we walked the sodden woods.
The tree trunks rose as columns
supporting the vaulted ceilings of branches.
Nature acted as our Holy Ghost.

Most of the year, the stream was a trickle.
The water table had fallen that low.
In the summer, sections sunk into mud,
more a swamp than a moving body
of water. But today, the skies
still dark, half gray, the first
of the sun faded, a real stream
flowed below our home.

If you remember, you said
we should find the pool
that formed after storms.
It was summer, and warm,
and we could soak our feet
in the cool water and watch
tiny fish nibble at our toes.

It was already hot and I wavered,
but you went uphill without me.
I watched you until I knew
you would not turn back.
We could go together,
or alone, in different ways.

On our way to that very spot,
you heard it first, or I did,
that low rumble, almost a hum,
of the waterfall, an echo, of a whisper,
as if some sylvan god,
or nymph, tried to advise us,
maybe to warn us not to go deeper.

Still, we went, deeper, into the trees.
You'd think the waterfall easy
to find: just follow the stream up
the incline. But the more we climbed,
the more distant, more distinct,
the sound became. By now, the sun
hung straight over the woods.

We waded through air more like water,
as if we were sea bottom explorers
searching for merchant wrecks
or lost ancient cities.

You paused and wiped the sweat
from your brow. I sat on a rotting log.
Together, we looked upward, to the sun
reaching through the leaves.
Dappled shadows danced across the ground.
Without a word, you turned back.
At the gravel drive
that led to the house, I said,
"Too bad we never saw the waterfall."
"We know what waterfalls are,"
you said. "We tried," I added.
"Satisfaction is in the trying."
You hmphed as you opened
the kitchen door. "I prefer
fantasy to struggle." The words
trickled off your tongue, as if
gravity forced them out.
You began to unlace
your mud-entombed boots.

Limestone

For millions of years, rainwater percolated through
    rotting leaves.
Turned acidic, it seeped through the cracks and
    fissures
of limestone bedrock, both solid and dissolvable.

Now, a lightless land, an anti-earth, lies underfoot the
    Ozarks.
When we walk the wooden paths of a state park,
or float beneath an overhang on a crystal stream,

we know, beneath us, is a world that both frightens
    and soothes.
Who hasn't stood at the mouth of a cave, and paused?
It's a deep fault within us, the twin wants, one to flee

into the sun, the other, to lose ourselves in the
    wandering darkness.
I think what draws us to caves is that what makes a
    cave
a cave is what is not there. We desire an ontology of
    absence.

But absence is one thing that can never be. This is
    what we fear:
our tears, turned bitter, wore away the certainty of
    any ground.

We are nothing more than caverns and karsts that
    crisscross

the fissures, crests, depressions, and ridges of our soft
    human form.
If even the earth cannot be trusted, how much less can
    we?
Maybe that is why we buried our dead in caves, to refill

this emptiness with human flesh and bone and winding
    sheets.
I like to believe that when we touch moist cave walls,
those are tears of the dead, in their decay, all the more
    solid.

White Washing

Near to Equality, black men ascended
enshrouded in rock salt from Saline Springs,
Illinois, then an admitted free state.

In hand-drawn river water, they washed off
the whiteness from their skin, picked whiteness from
beneath their nails, blew white snot from their noses,

coughed up what they jokingly called "white lung"
before they fried their cornmeal in fatback
then passed around a new tobacco plug

and swapped tall tales until the hearth fire died.
A station on the Reverse Underground
Railroad, Equality sold more than salt.

So many things can be kept for so long
if you pack them in salt and let them age.
Reconstituted, they return to new.

Today, the state owns Equality's Old Slave House,
where Lincoln spoke on the second floor. Slave
pens, twelve in all, formed the floor above him.

An odd quiet muffled the great man's speech.
Many ears longed to be filled with such words.
The home is closed for pending renovation.

Instead, tourists can wander through the Garden
of the Gods, in Shawnee National Forest,
named after a people who once lived there.

Still Water

On the bone-bleached sands of the leeward keys,
I look outward, to the roiling rollers
with seductive tides that undermine

any sense of permanent place. Maps, no matter
how accurate, are always wrong.
The land does not end here,

the sea there, an easy demarcation
between the solid and the unreliable.
If the modern Tarot of facts and figures

reads well, plats of the future will be blue
with submerged cities, drowned farmers,
coasts along the shortgrass steppe.

A laceration of pus-colored clouds opens
above the pale surf. Further out,
the putrid swell breaks into the spray.

I wade into the troubled water. A purple flag
flutters above the guard shack.
The threat of danger skulks

beneath the combers. A palmful of grit,
quartz and feldspar sifts
through my fingers, wrinkled

by water into a tangible topography
of abysmal plains and seamounts.
I carry an ocean in my hand.

A longing rises within me. I do not like the sea,
but it baits me with its traps, its mysteries,
darkness, seemingly unfathomable depth.

What if I, like a suicide, enter the spindrift, and swim,
out, and out, further, until my strength
dissolves, I sink, becoming my own jetsam,

as if abandoning myself is my salvation, or,
like lagan, I rest on the ocean floor,
until ebb and flow wash me on the strand?

Whiskey River

Some prisons are their own escape. As memory
pours itself into its own Platonic forms,

our recollections make the past, not recognize it.
That's why whiskey is a magical genie. Rethinking

becomes free form, as Willie Nelson sang, partially
right. The whiskey river takes us, yet we do not drown,

but like runaways confused about the compass points,
float downriver, some of us Huck, others Jim.

We don't often get to choose. I tell myself,
when I pour a fourth small nip of a bottle I saved,

in theory, for others: Huck chose Hell and the West.
Jim? What exactly did Jim choose? To be decent.

I select a $50 bourbon and the Midwest. Twain
would have understood. There is only so much

America a white person can stomach. Before vomiting,
experts say drink water. Mine is from the Mississippi.

When you add water to whiskey, the oil separates,
floats on top in small threads, like the yarns

river boatmen told, or the slicks at the refinery
near Wood River, where Lewis and Clark first camped

for the winter before poling their commission upstream.
My privilege is that my freedom resides in a bottle.

stone
stone
stone
stone

Retaining Walls

Along the far edge of the parking lot
the landlord's men stacked rough-hewn stone to build
a retaining wall for the runoff rain.

Before the backhoe gouged the ground and broke
the asphalt's lip, a picket fence, of sorts,
stood sentry around the dumpster and cars,

the kind of fence I could imagine settlers
built to keep their culture in as much as keep
unconquered wilderness out, they'd thought.

Like all intended boundaries, the fence fell
into disrepair. Spring rain, winter freeze
did their harm with rusted nails, rotted wood.

Along the cornerstone, a divide opened,
a makeshift gate, that allowed a bypass
from the potholed drive on the outer side.

A neighbor boy would pedal his bike through
then abandon it next to the back steps.
To my amazement, it was never stolen.

His mom shortcut her way from car to door
with full grocery bags and calls to him
to hurry and help her up the rear hall.

Even I once pushed through the split balusters
but tripped and caught my hand on splintered wood.
I learned not to stray from the ordained path.

The workmen blocked my spot with cut and fill,
and kept the clay dirt and severed tree roots
within the yellow lines. The work was right,

I had to admit. A new wall was needed.
Bounds must be set, what is in, what is out.
Old ways are abandoned. They always are.

With all the talk of more walls in the news,
it was foreseeable for me to think
of tearing down old walls, building new ones.

There's some thing about walls that comforts me,
like a father who defines family rules,
or common sense, or just the way things are.

I observed the men crenellate the cope
and implant PVC pipe for weep holes
and lay deadmen at right angles as anchors,

and I thought of letters, and words, and lines,
the comfort that comes with structure and form.
Even chaos relies on definition.

There's an allure to chaos, isn't there,
temptation that without God one can will
anything? We all like that sort of lie.

The building manager has apologized
to me: the retaining wall took too long.
The men should've finished by now, but haven't.

And I'm OK with that. Not all our walls
are meant to last. Maybe none of them are.
Yet, there is something about walls I love.

Malls

China has its Wall. Europe, its Versailles.
Egypt touts its Pyramids. Peru, its Inca Trail.
We have our malls, named for directions—
Northwest, South County, Mid-Rivers—
as if without them we couldn't find ourselves.

Malls have their own architecture:
Imhotep's columns at the entrance;
shops in-line like the Agora of Athens;
fountains, plants, even fish fit
for the atrium of a Roman villa.

The past was always on sale at malls.
First dates. Hastily bought birthday presents.
Engagement rings. Any Friday night.
Prom dresses and tuxes. Even weddings.
Like Santa, life was staged.

But like parents we no longer visit,
unless we need something, they aged.
When we saw them last, how shocked
we were. The emptiness of it all.
Their wornness. Then they were gone.

It seems trivial to make so much of malls.
And it is, if we remember the trivium
was a crossroads, a meeting place,
where people, like you and me, made
lives. We could've done worse than a mall.

Diners

Sing Hestia of crispy hashbrowns,
buttered wheat toast, of eggs
any way you like, stale black coffee,
Tabasco sprinkled like holy water.

These are the eucharist of a most holy office.
Salt and pepper shakers, sugar casters,
the sacred vessels of the ordinary form
of this American congregation

of men, almost always men, who greet
with grunts and nods and dry words
of sports or weather or the torments of the flesh.
They all drink the same bitter cup.

I've seen them, at 2 am, the gay couple,
the drunk teen, the fat trucker,
the waitress with a beehive who tells you
what you'll order, the short-order cook.

We make cautious, unsettled chitchat,
hash out a few of the world's problems,
lament the destruction of the nation,
nod "so be it," then eat in silence.

With names like Courtesy, Cornerstone,
Eat-Rite, The Palace, Whitey's,
only the décor changes. The menu, like life,
follows liturgies. That is why we came.

Names

When I push a sprout into the earth,
or mound soil atop a handful of seed,
I memorize the plot I've laid out,
though I know, in the end, I'll forget.

So, in the shed, I notate each square,
the what, the when, the where, the how,
as if I were inscribing a creation myth
for some future fool to read and cherish.

That was my first mistake. I draw a blank
on the meaning of my own words,
and interpret, as if it were arcane,
my own writing. So much for scripture.

With black marker and paper cards,
I staked the things in the garden.
A graveyard of popsicle sticks
defined the furrow and mounds.

The first rain washed my handiwork away.
That was my second mistake, to believe
writing prevented oblivion. In any form,
words become visions we see but cannot touch.

I gave up my ghost, and the garden grew
how it willed, contrary and nonconforming.
Orange squash bloomed. Tomato vines climbed.
Carrot stems frizzed. Onion stalks waved

like congregants beset by the Spirit.
I knew what I'd sown only when I reaped.
Consequences reveal the cause.
Endings explicate beginnings.

I put those ideas to rest.
The squirrels left tomatoes half-eaten.
The pinky-sized carrots went to seed.
I stuffed the squash blooms with cream cheese
and already plot next spring plantings.

Rhizomes

The more I dig, the more I find.
The ground that I live upon is full
of junk: coins, wires, screws, a key,
shards of glass, a swatch of cloth,
a jaundiced scrap of cardboard
with smudged handwriting.
With each step, I press upon
buried histories, forgotten lives.

But that's not why I dig
hard Missouri clay
that masquerades as my lawn.
I probe for rootstalks,
confused stems that do not stretch
downward, to water, or upward,
to the sun, but side to side,
each in search of the other.

Maybe that's been my misstep,
seeing movement only
up, to the heavens, to the light,
or down, to darkness,
and chambers and passageways.
I never learned to look,
like the cross, left or right,
but stayed blind to others

beside me. Tribulations and trials
shared, if never spoken,
weave networks between us.
No one can find them all,
I conclude, as I rip a cord of root
from one node to another.
Unearthing connections is endless.
I leave that work for another day.

Charnel

When I dream of letters, I dream
bones, blackened ancient bones
in my charnel house of words,

bones long, short, flat, twisted,
stacked neatly in lines, as if death
were orderly. Skulls are separated.

My fingers read ridges and grooves,
cuneiform of pasts I refuse to admit
are past. I am a collector of bones.

I am not alone in amassing bones.
In Cambodia, there are millions.
In the sewers of Paris, even more.

In Austria, they paint flowers on them.
Yogis find them transgressive, like sex.
Monks stack new bones under Mt. Sinai.

You, too, reader, add my bones
to the ossuary of your mind
where you may wander, at night,

and contemplate your own brief life.
Only those of us enslaved to bones
dream of a freedom begotten from them.

Silence

The hour before a storm, the birds fall silent
and cluster in trees or along the ground
or roost on rafters of abandoned barns.

That's how we know, before the sky grows dark,
the putrid scent of coming rain, or hair
that stands on end, we have a squall in hand.

Like this, I imagine our time of death
a hush, the echoes of memory faded,
then lightning, thunder, death rattle, the end.

After the passing clouds, birds sing again.
The air is clean. The neighbor's children play
in puddles. Oil forms rainbows in the street.

Attis

It was a time of drought
when the land was neither
living nor dead, not asleep,
yet not awake, fallow, soulless.

A crucified scarecrow hung
on two crossed staves.
Cans dangling on strings thudded.
Crows picked at the straw man's eyes.

This summer, sighs were frequent.
You would not think the drought
undid so many. Haboobs heaped
fogs of sand onto summer dawns.

Families planted their generations
in wrought-iron fenced plots.
In spring, no corpses sprouted.
Last year was the last fruit to bear.

The priest mixed his water and wine,
dipped his unleavened bread.
A grandma shuffled her cards.
She chose the Jack of Hearts

as her trump. She envied death.
At her age, the past is all she knew.
Her family crumbled like dry soil.
"We never rebelled against God,"

she prayed. A plastic rosary bit
between her fingers. "But were we
faithful?" It was America in which
they had trusted. Hearts trump all.

The county is named for a forgotten
general, the town, a wiped-out tribe.
Soon, all the land will be corporate.
We all live in colonized souls.

A hooded man rapped the door.
Or so it seemed. Only the sheriff,
a good man, the next town over,
delivered a sheaf of legal papers.

In the barn, her son, the tiller
of the fields, blew his head off.
A perverse onanist, he spilt
his blood upon the ground.

Mound City

Olive-hued Pierre Laclede stepped from the mud-
  tone river
to an even browner bank. It is recorded he owned
  five
Indians as slaves.

Hundreds of mounds checkered the bluffs above
  the landing.
One by one, like stumps in an unplowed field,
settlers uprooted and flattened the land.

There are no mounds left in the city, except one,
south of the brewery. The Osage own it, though,
they do not claim it as their own.

On the American Bottom, a mound as large as Giza
rose to the sky. Trappists gardened on its terraces.
The mound is named after these priests.

This is Cahokia. The largest mound collapses
from the inside. The state will not pay for upkeep.
A Peoria killed a Pontiac near there.

In one burial mound, over one hundred young girls,
strangled or bludgeoned, accompanied a great chief,
or priest, one assumes, to heaven.

Today, between Cahokia and The Gateway Arch,
Waste Management, Inc., has built a mound,
over 200 acres, within the arms

of an ox-bow lake, as if nature tries
to contain human history. You can see
this mound from space.

Sleeping Volcanoes

In southeast Missouri, there are sleeping volcanoes,
true mountains birthed when magma cleaved
the mantle and expelled the afterbirth of ash,

lava, and gas. The state owns those mountains now.
Along with a handful of corporations
of modern alchemy smelting lead to gold.

Families with babies, friends with beers, lovers
hand-in-hand, schoolchildren in single file,
hike across the dome, hardened over time.

None of them contemplate, even acknowledge,
the fire beneath their soles. This fire, too, sleeps,
a Behemoth, bent on one day reemerging

from an eon of hibernation. If from ash we came,
then, perhaps, we will return to fine tephra.
Like falling angels, we will pall the earth.

I often wonder what is hidden beneath our annealed
    skins,
our cloaks, masks, cosmetics, personae?
When we smooth our fingertips across

another's nose, mouth, forehead, lips, is this not
topography formed by violence, stress,
fault, fissure, this landscape we name our face?

Flyover Dharma

From thirty thousand feet, the Midwest appears
     manicured.
Sutures of interstate knit a patchwork of fields
into a cover fitted for a king, or mighty prophet.

As if they were stones placed in a raked gravel courtyard,
farmhouses, barns, silos sit perfectly among the furrows.
Soy and corn sway like seiche in a temple pond.

At that height, even the rivers run orderly beside their
     levees,
as if locks and dams were natural cataracts,
and brick-lined wharfs, nothing but sun-baked sand.

Each time I leave, I am certain I will never return,
     though one way
always leads to another way. There is no end to going.
Homecoming is simply the stop after another departure,

before the next announcement the door will close and
     not reopen.
I cannot sit like this for long. Knees lock. Back aches.
     Head throbs.
Diet Coke and Biscoff cookies are a sparse offering

for my suffering. The attendant offers me kind words,
     as if her speech
were a mantra, her smile a tantra to ward away demons.
If I am already a buddha, then the world failed to notice.

Through the window, my eyes devour a landscape of
    endless sky. For me,
the clouds are like shoaling white horses breaking
    on shallows.
But, it is me who moves. The world stands still,
    and waits.

Territoriality

This spring dawn, birds begin their cacophony of chants,
all sex and violence, imprints of who will rule the yard,
whose offspring's offspring will populate this patch of
   earth.

The morning traffic, too, has its cries, trills, alarms,
   greetings,
rich or thin, metallic, harsh, calls for submission, and
   dominance
over the interwoven nest of roads, ways, signals, and
   signs.

Great American Desert

There is no water but only sandy, calcareous soil,
and no trees to fell for a lean-to, or to hang a noose.

Abandoned buffalo wallows gather stagnant pools.
Tendrils of creeks pass as rivers. They make no
    sound.

The only sound is the wind, always the wind,
as if a drunk God had forgotten how to be silent.

Come south of the mountains, warm desert winds
    breed
with the cold air of the north. They birth tempests.

Maybe it's how the mountains subdue the sky,
alter its jet streams, shade its sun, impede its views

of unbroken horizons, maybe these are why storms
bloom into yellows and purples and greens and blues,

with clouds that seem to tumble over each other,
as if above us were an Edenic formal flower garden

fenced, furrowed, and sown by a maniacal bachelor
who breeds hybrids, lives with cats, and breathes dust.

As for me, I feel more awe than fear at a prairie storm.
The child in me excites, as if a father, gone to war,

has returned, more myth than man, with the rage
only men too hurt to know pain carry as a fetish.

With such a brooding nature, a squall line entices:
"Come. Trust me. In my violence is freedom."

In a derecho, the rain parallels the earth.
Droplets sting like miniature flint arrowheads.

Trees rip from their roots. Walls topple like sticks.
Streets back up with sewage. Lives turn upside down.

But it is the peace after the storm that admonishes.
We do not often hear what the silence says.

When I listen, what does it say? That true silence
does not exist. There is always a whisper in the air,

a prophecy that in a world of unbroken vision,
there is also life to lose, and life to make.

That is what one finds here, among the scrub
and shortgrass. Silence is another order of voice.

Leadbelt

Trends of lead, silver, copper, and zinc
vein the middle of Missouri. Precious
or base, the DNR holds dominion.

For centuries, Missouri lead fed the muzzles
of European wars, then American,
then world. Across the river, in Alton,

where a mob hanged the abolitionist Lovejoy,
Winchester Ammunition carries
this earthly past into a too-human future.

Empire gave way to republic, like a plot of land
called by a different name because of forms
filed with the recorder of deeds.

In time, new mines bored into the rock.
Others closed and flooded with weep
from the smooth-hewn longwalls.

Today, one mine, so aptly named Bonne Terre,
is the world's largest underground lake.
Scuba divers flutter like naiads

through rooms filled with the rusted bodies
of machines, rotted carcasses
of Leviathans, reminders even gods die.

Flare

On certain summer nights, with clouds flooded
along the horizon, the slot oven doors
opened and exposed the airless kilns

where coal, the petrified bodies of the dead
sunk to the bed of a salt sea once
spread across these Midwest plains,

hardens into gray and porous raw coke.
The coral glow of the blast furnace
reflected off the mirror-sea sky

as if a midnight sunrise countered the rotation
of the earth and Midwest aurora dazzled
the expanse of steel works and staging yards

and tired eyes in tar-paper shacks and dim-lit bars.
Like a perverted obelisk, a flare stack glows
a Pentecost-blue flame of methane and tar.

Those who work beneath the fire are grateful.
Their children gasp for breath and die young.
We always burn off what we cannot value.

Descansos

Along the interstates and county roads,
you see them, makeshift crosses, rudely nailed
slats, painted white, leaning, as if exhausted.

Bouquets of plastic flowers, photographs,
sun-bleached, rain-warped, and plush stuffed
    animals,
in silence, huddle, like saints beneath the cross

and remind us there's life after our death.
Others will carry our names in their mouths.
For some, even strangers know where they died.

I've never raised a cross on a thin shoulder,
beyond the solid line and rumble strips,
where the grass slopes down to the frontage road,

yet, they move me, these monuments to grief
and love. I wonder what were their names, age,
their favorite food. I never stop to look.

These shrines are meant for us, the passersby,
we who speed headlong to unchosen ends.
They remind us that all loss should be shared.

I keep them with me, interred in the lines
of this poem, words you read, take with you,
words we all hold, 'til we come to our rest.

Wrecking

For me, they are sea wrecks on shallow shoals,
the vehicles askew in drainage ditches,
sometimes beyond the frontage road barbed wire,
or left on hard shoulders as derelicts.

Windshield wipers are often bent at angles.
The sliding doors of minivans are off
their rails. The flanks of sedans are ripped open
by Jaws of Life. Others are burnt-out shells.

Their histories are treasures for my mind.
Like a deep-sea diver, I mask my face
and salvage what I think are lives, deaths, fears.
Imagined compassion is as good as gold,

when one is poor in spirit, and bereft
of love. The problem, for me, for us, is,
in abstract, love for all is a salt sea
that buoys us against our own dead weight.

The concrete world is the hazard: guardrails;
no passing solid lines; limited sight;
a pause at a stop sign a bit too long;
a lane change without the required blinker.

The gears of love are indexed in inverse:
the greater love of humanity, less
the love of each human. Maybe that is
why we strain our necks, bare our eyes to see

passing wrecks. A compassionate moment
gives reprieve to those grinding brakes inside,
the gnash of real against ideal, the fact
we will someday be another's wrecked pity.

Thomasson

Where once a rotted wood balcony stood,
a second-floor door opened to the air
on the back facade of the Tic and Toc Speakeasy.
Green and pink, with red shades, the door was new.
The glass was clean. The doorknob polished brass
no hand would turn. Some steps are left untaken.
We keep so much of life for no true use:
friendships; jobs; marriages; homes; even dreams
of what was, could be. This door is not false,
but prompts remembrance of the past, the lost,
and offers futures we can choose, or not.
At least this is the story we prefer.
I like that door. Not all beautiful things
need purpose. Some things are best left to be.

Tornado Alley

In the Book of Revelation, archangels posted
at the imagined corners of the globe.
They held back the four winds of the earth,

but must have abandoned this plot of flat land
between Appalachia and the Rockies.
Here, the winds master the beasts of the fields.

If you've seen a tornado, you can only think of a god,
intemperate, implacable, a contradiction
turning inwards. We live outside this violence

that bridges sky and ground, a pillar of clouds
in the sparsely treed expanses of prairie.
At least here, there is scant forbidden fruit.

With each passing storm season, we remember
that we are an unsettled people. Canaanite
or Hebrew, either way, tornados flatten crops,

tear roofs from wood-frame houses, snap telephone
    poles,
and, like words from a prophet, collapse the hubris
from the lullaby that soothes the heart of a country.

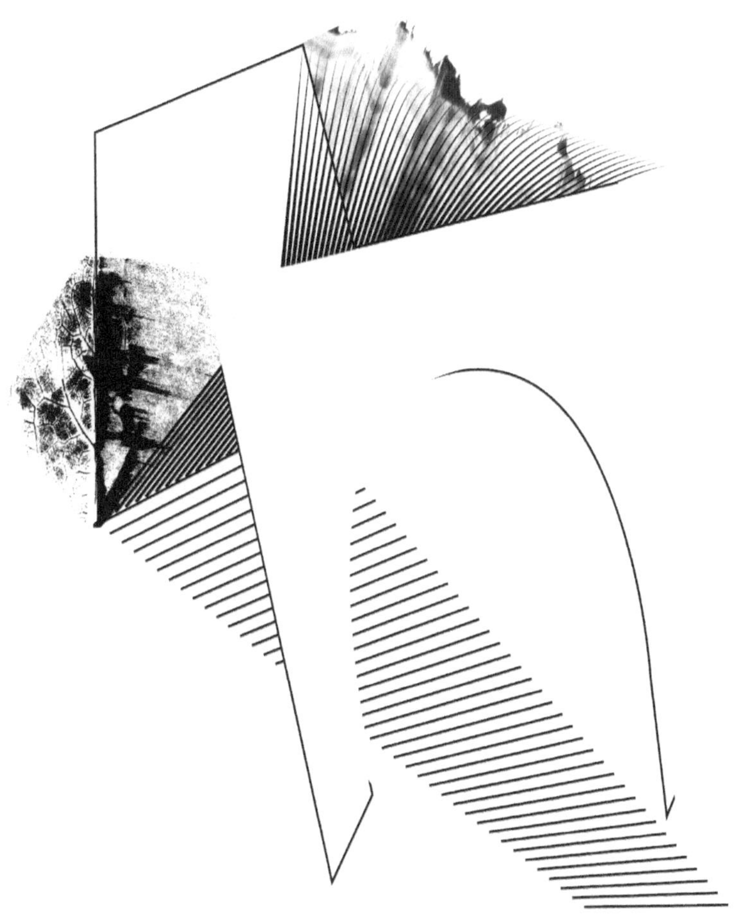

Continental Drift

The earth always moves beneath us,
though we think our standpoint still.

Here, in the stolid Midwest, we drift
westward, southward, one inch per year.

When I turned fifty, where I was born
was nearly fifty feet from where it had been.

Plats must be dismantled; distances, redrawn.
How are any of us to know where we are?

Once, years ago, here in the land of rivers,
the earth shook us to our bones.

Church bells rang in Boston. The river
ran backwards, a metaphor for time.

We haven't had such a scare since,
though experts warn: expect change soon.

The country under my feet is shifting.
The center stays the center, yet moves.

There is no fixed thing as entropy,
only new patterns, yet unmeasured.

Words, like land in an earthquake,
become liquid. Meaning is infinite.

When I trace my finger along a map,
I am a child drawing in sea-swept sand.

The map is paper. It's geography, ink.
I live in a land I no longer recognize.

Counting Coup

Newspapers predict a blow to the state,
the constitution in tatters and shreds.
Someone should act. It's almost too late.

There were quotes like this, by an American great:
'The only good ones are the ones who are dead,"
Newspapers quoted. A strike at the State

of the Union ended the other debate.
Then the bullet in Lincoln's head.
Someone should have acted. It was too late.

"Change takes time. You'll have your turn. Just wait."
Then dogs, fire hoses. The rivers flowed red.
Newspapers ran photos from Southern states,

the Levant, the Sahil, the Orient.
"There will be investigations by the Feds.
"Someone should act, before it's too late,"

the Senator said. They say love, not hate,
conquers all. The thought fills me with dread.
The media still predicts a blow to the state.
Someone acted. Others waited too late.

Field Work

I slave under the summer sun.
My skin grows dark.
Like the fading of my own shadow,
black in my self-image, I root
deep into the topsoil, full of crops
I judiciously garden: ebony blue of eggplant;
green of collard and turnip; uncircumcised
shafts of okra; chthonic white flesh of the yam.

I take refuge in this abstract survey
of the earth, a form of real estate I own.
Land is not chattel that can steal
away in the night. What is mine is mine.
The law confirms in me as much.
I have my piece. What more
is there for any of us?

That is how I seed the world.
There is no truth above the law.
Yet, I suspect there are bodies buried
in these raised beds, tombs
of board and nail and joint.
If I dig, I fear to find ossified history.
I am pale like bones.
My sin is indifference.

Beyond my garden wall, injustice
spreads its rhizomes, pushes bitter
roots downward, noxious stems to the skies.
I cannot keep this construct at bay;
a part must be of the whole. As I weed,
my mind wanders, through the gate,
down the path, up the street, to what
this country life, this heart of the heart
of the country, might have been,
given different sowing.

But that is the garden of mine own
imagination: each, separate, equal,
has an owned plot of land.
Ownership is freedom.
We know we must believe so.
This is a harvest worthy of tender.
I test the fullness of this yield's fruit,
select the good from the bad.
In the fall, my darkness fades.
I will sleep through the snow,
hidden from the fading winter sun.

Milkweed

When I was young, tapestries of milkweed
intertwined with the knitted steel wire chain-link
that armored the backyard. After rain,
the milkweed pods burst. Silky threads of seed
spilled upon the earth. Latex sap would bleed
down the hairy stem. Each fall, in a vain
try to uproot the herb, my dad would strain
at covert rhizomes. But nature would cede
no ground. Now, the milkweed is near extinct,
except in my mind, where wild gardens raise
images of the past. Isn't all the past
a metaphor? Everything known is linked.
Beyond this lattice of words is a vast
wasteland of things that frighten and amaze.

Murmuration

In Midwest winters, at the early dusk,
starlings give rise to babbling brooks of wings
that wend through skies treeless as open plains.

The birds recircle, eddy, boil, corkscrew
across imaginary beds of rock
clouds white as granite worn smooth to the touch.

No center holds. No shape persists. The flock
expands until it floods over the banks
that bound the gray-lit twilight bottomland.

I close my eyes and hear murmurs of gods
when they flock above me. What do they say,
these synchronized auspices of the divine?

At crest, stretched across the glacial horizons,
the chattering at last settles on fields
of corn stubble beneath a cold full moon.

Touch

Brush your palm across
the weather-worn edge
of a grave marker,

trace a fingertip
along chiseled
names and dates,

you will decipher
a passage of time
by uneven stone.

So much history
there is to know
through touch.

Outline the eyes,
the nose, the mouth,
of a sleeping child,

smooth your cheek
against the leathered
face of a grandfather,

our biographies are writ
on our skin, past, future,
stretched taut across us.

Componere

The dead we loved do not live within us, as if we
    were abandoned frames
with broken panes of glass and splintered clapboard
    shingles
that fluttered in strong winds until they peeled like
    sunburnt skin.
We are not the smoothed granite of mortise and tenon
    crypt walls,
or battlefields with adjoining graves, or asylums,
    hospitals, or orphan homes.
Our bodies are not the places where the dead choose
    to dwell,
with our sticky arteries and arthritic vertebrae that creak
    like uneven floorboards.
Only those lost, or who want to be lost, sleep in
    ramshackle huts.

Even if we light candles before icon-like images set on
    a living room shelf,
or leave our oblationary tears on the grass that surrounds
    their gravestones,
or page through a photo album and recollect from a
    faint image
that one Sunday, at the park, when it rained, and
    something
happened, but what, something, or the trip out of town
    with things

gone all wrong, but we were happy then, or those
    singular traits
we hated, but now that the other is dead, and we,
    alone, we long for them.
What have the dead left of themselves for us but
    ash and spectral memory?

Imagine that each of us is our own earth, with our
    own molten core, with seas
that rise and fall by the thaw and freeze of ice,
    distinct fauna, flora,
eons, eras, periods, epochs. If you know your
    science, you know the dead
are the stuff of our own bodies: the calcium in our
    bones; the iron
in our blood; the oxygen that gives us mass; the
    carbon that gives us form.
The dead do not sleep in us, but they are in us, their
    decomposed selves.
Imagine if we mine the veins that striate our tissues,
    or drill blast holes in our bones,
or crater the flat surface of our skin, as if we were
    contractors in search

of rare substances demanded by our insatiable
    needs. We extract our desire handful
by handful from the pit of our stomach and the
    bowels of our loins.
We separate and process and crush and grind the
    dead who make us whole.

Our wills are machines engineered to move our
    thoughts from then
to now. When we study ourselves or study our past,
    both being equal, we find
that we are always one step behind ourselves. The
    present moment
is that last mortgage payment coupon that reappears
    the next month, untorn,
the perforation intact, the free-and-clear deed always
    one installment away.

No, the dead do not rest within us, nor do we arise in
    the dead. They and we are
one, as the past, present, and future unite into the
    abstraction called time.
Think of a house, in the middle of the Midwest plains,
    wood frame, timber from Maine,
asphalt roofing from Michigan, lead pipes from St.
    Louis, all delivered
by boxcar, care of Sears & Roebuck. Then the stove
    flue creosote catches fire.
Days later, the family sifts through the warm embers
    for the remnants of their lives.
That house will rot, as we will. The untreated wood will
    degrade into humus.
Somewhere, something, someone, will absorb those
    remains and live.

Wild Violets

We find them between the ties of hushed rails,
or cracked schoolyard blacktops,
even between control joints of sidewalks
that bank an abandoned city street,
the discarded things of human hand,
the undesired, uprooted, burnt
by controlled flame, or shorn
against summer dust.

Midwest yards harbor them,
delicate, beautiful,
as if heaven, filled with stars,
scattered across zoysia,
a cloudless sky in negative,
the grass, endless space,
the blooms, darkened stars,
and we, angels in our glory.

Their persistence is what frightens me,
cultivated, urbane, refined,
righting words in straight furrows
as if orderliness, being in itself,
gives rise against nature's ordered chaos,
takes root in the measured gardens,
earth turned under plow,
each spring planting given to its fall.

Yet, I love them so much.
Those things we name weeds,
in their uncommon plainness,
unplanned, unintended,
comfort me in deep-rooted knowing
that after the plotting, and platting,
the unconceived, the un-engendered,
will cover our feral desire.

Richard Stimac lives in the St. Louis, Missouri (USA) area. He has published a poetry book *Bricolage* (Spartan Press), two poetry chapbooks, and one flash fiction chapbook. In his work, Richard explores time and memory through the landscape and humanscape of the St. Louis region. He invites you to follow his poetry Facebook page: "Richard Stimac poet".

Ladan Bahmani and **Brian Patrick Franklin** are artists and designers whose collaborative practice overlaps image and language to explore how meaning takes shape, dissolves, and reforms. Their installations and printed works have drawn on the tension between analog and digital artistic techniques, as well as traditions of illuminated manuscripts that reference their Persian and Irish backgrounds. They have exhibited their work in solo exhibitions, including Chaotic & Harmonious at the St. Louis Artists' Guild, For Those Who Don't Yet Have the Words at Auburn University, and Sometimes There, Sometimes Not at the University of Michigan Hospital Gallery.

Bahmani holds an MFA in Graphic Design from Michigan State University and a BS in Graphic Design from South Dakota State University. Franklin holds an MFA in New Media from Pennsylvania State University and a BFA in Media Arts from the State University of New York at Fredonia. They teach graphic design and digital fabrication courses in the Wonsook Kim School of Art at Illinois State University.

This project was made possible, in part, by generous support from the Osage Arts Community.

Osage Arts Community provides temporary time, space and support for the creation of new artistic works in a retreat format, serving creative people of all kinds — visual artists, composers, poets, fiction and nonfiction writers. Located on a 152-acre farm in an isolated rural mountainside setting in Central Missouri and bordered by ¾ of a mile of the Gasconade River, OAC provides residencies to those working alone, as well as welcoming collaborative teams, offering living space and workspace in a country environment to emerging and mid-career artists. For more information, visit us at www.osageac.org

www.ingramcontent.com/pod-product-compliance
Lightning Source LLC
Chambersburg PA
CBHW062143150726
47991CB00006B/2155